# Tertullian
## On Exhortation to Chastity

# Tertullian
# On Exhortation to Chastity

# Tertullian
# On Exhortation to Chastity

© Lighthouse Publishing 2018

All rights reserved. Without limiting the rights under copyright reserved above, no part of this publication may be reproduced, stored in a retrieval system, or transmitted, in any form or by any means (electronic, mechanical, photocopying, recording or otherwise), without the prior written permission of the copyright owner of this book.

Published by
Lighthouse Christian Publishing
SAN 257-4330
5531 Dufferin Drive
Savage, Minnesota, 55378
United States of America

www.lighthousechristianpublishing.com

# Tertullian

## On Exhortation to Chastity.

Chapter I.—Introduction. Virginity Classified Under Three Several Species.

I doubt not, brother, that after the premission in peace of your wife, you, being wholly bent upon the composing of your mind (to a right frame), are seriously thinking about the end of your lone life, and of course are standing in need of counsel. Although, in cases of this kind, each individual ought to hold colloquy with his own faith, and consult its strength; still, inasmuch as, in this (particular) species (of trial), the *necessity of the flesh* (which generally is faith's antagonist at the bar of the same inner consciousness, to which I have alluded) sets cogitation astir, faith has need of counsel from without, as an advocate, as it were, to oppose the *necessities of the flesh*: which necessity, indeed, may very easily be circumscribed, if the *will* rather than the *indulgence* of God be considered. No one deserves (favor) by availing himself of the indulgence, but by rendering a prompt obedience to the will, (of his master). The will of God is our sanctification, for He wishes His "image"—us—to become likewise His "likeness;" that we may be "holy" just as Himself is "holy." That good—sanctification, I mean—I distribute into several species, that in some one of those species we may be found. The first species is, virginity from one's birth: the second, virginity from one's *second* birth, that is, from the font; which (second virginity) either in the marriage state keeps (its subject) pure by mutual compact, or else perseveres in widowhood from choice: a third grade remains, monogamy, when, after the interception of a marriage once contracted, there is thereafter a renunciation of sexual connection. The first virginity is (the virginity) of happiness, (and consists in) total ignorance of that from which you will afterwards wish to be freed: the second, of virtue, (and consists in) contemning that the power of which you know full well: the remaining species, (that) of marrying no more after the disjunction of matrimony by death, besides being the glory of virtue, is (the glory) of moderation likewise; for moderation is the not regretting a thing which has been taken away, and taken away by the Lord God, without whose will neither does a leaf glide down from a tree, nor a sparrow of one farthing's worth fall to the earth.

## Chapter II. —The Blame of Our Misdeeds Not to Be Cast Upon God. The One Power Which Rests with Man is the Power of Volition.

What moderation, in short, is there in that utterance, "The Lord gave, the Lord hath taken away; as seemed (good) to the Lord, so hath it been done!" And accordingly, if we renew nuptials which have been taken away, doubtless we strive against the will of God, willing to have over again a thing which He has not willed us to have. For had He willed (that we should), He would not have taken it away; unless we interpret this, too, to be the will of God, as if He again willed us to have what He just now did not will. It is not the part of good and solid faith to refer all things to the will of God in such a manner as that; and that each individual should so flatter himself by saying that "nothing is done without His permission,"

as to make us fail to understand that there is a something in our own power. Else every sin will be excused if we persist in contending that nothing is done by us without
the will of God; and that definition will go to the destruction of (our) whole discipline, (nay), even of God Himself; if either He produce by His own will things which He wills not, or else (if) there is nothing which God wills not. But as there are some things which He forbids, against which He denounces even eternal punishment—for, of course, things which He *forbids*, and by which withal He is *offended*, He does not *will*—so too, on the contrary, what He *does* will, He enjoins and sets down as acceptable, and repays with the reward of eternity. And so, when we have learnt from His precepts each (class of actions), what He does not will and what He does, we still have a volition and an arbitrating power of electing the one; just as it is written, "Behold, I have set before thee good and evil: for thou hast tasted of the tree of knowledge." And accordingly we ought not to lay to the account of the Lord's will that which lies subject to our own choice; (on the hypothesis) that He does not will, or else (positively) nills what is good, who does nill what is evil. Thus, it is a volition of our own when we will what is evil, in antagonism to God's will, who wills what is good. Further, if you inquire whence comes that volition whereby we will anything in antagonism to the will of God, I shall say, it has its source in ourselves. And I shall not make the assertion rashly—for you must needs correspond to the seed whence you spring—if indeed it be true, (as it is), that the originator of our race and our sin, Adam, willed the sin which he committed. For the devil did not impose upon him the volition to sin, but sub ministered material to the volition. On the other hand, the will of God had come to be a question of obedience. In like manner you, too, if you fail to obey God, who has trained you by setting before you the precept of free action, will, through the liberty of your will, willingly turn into the downward course of doing what God nills: and thus you think yourself to have been subverted by the devil; who, albeit he does *will* that you should

will something which God nills still does not *make* you will it, inasmuch as he did not *reduce* those our protoplasts
to the volition of sin; nay, nor (did *reduce* them at all) against their will, or in ignorance as to what God nilled. For, of course, He nilled (a thing) to be done when He made death the destined consequence of its commission. Thus the work of the devil is one: to make trial whether you do will that which it rests with you to will. But when you *have* willed, it follows that he subjects you to himself; not by having *wrought* volition in you, but by having found a favorable opportunity in your volition. Therefore, since the only thing which is in our power is volition—and it is herein that our mind toward God is put to proof, whether we will the things which coincide with His will—deeply and anxiously must the will of God be
pondered again and again, I say, (to see) what even in *secret* He may will.

Chapter III. —Of Indulgence and Pure Volition. The Question Illustrated.

For what things are *manifest* we all know; and *in what sense* these very things are manifest must be thoroughly examined. For, albeit some things seem to savor of "the will
of God," seeing that they are *allowed* by Him, it does not forthwith follow that everything which is *permitted* proceeds out of the mere and absolute will of him who permits. *Indulgence* is the source of all *permission*. And albeit indulgence is not independent of volition, still, inasmuch as it has its *cause* in him to whom the indulgence is granted, it comes (as it were) from *unwilling* volition, having experienced a producing cause of itself which *constrains* volition. See what is the nature of a volition of which some second party is the cause. There is, again, a second species of *pure* volition to be considered. God wills us to do some acts pleasing to Himself, in which it is not indulgence which patronizes, but discipline which lords it. If, however, He has given a preference over

these to some other acts—(acts), of course, which He *more* wills—is there a doubt that the acts which we are to pursue are those which He *more* wills; since those which He *less* wills (because He wills others *more*) are to be similarly regarded as if He did *not* will them? For, by showing what He *more* wills, He has effaced the lesser volition by the greater. And in as far as He has proposed each (volition) to your knowledge, in so far has He defined it to be your duty to pursue that which He has declared that He *more* wills. Then, if the object of His declaring has been that you may pursue that which He *more* wills; doubtless, unless you do so, you savor of contrariety to His volition, by savoring of contrariety to His *superior* volition; and you rather offend than merit reward, by doing what He wills indeed, and rejecting what He *more* wills. Partly, you sin; partly, if you sin not, still you deserve no reward. Moreover, is not even the unwillingness to deserve reward a sin?

If, therefore, second marriage finds the source of its allowance in that "will of God" which is called indulgence, we shall deny that that which has indulgence for its cause is volition pure; if in that to which some other—that, namely, which regards continence as more desirable—is preferred as superior, we shall have learned (by what has been argued above), that the not-superior is rescinded by the superior. Suffer me to have touched upon these considerations, in order that I may now follow the course of the apostle's words. But, in the first place, I shall not be thought irreligious if I remark on what he himself professes; (namely), that he has introduced all *indulgence* in regard to marriage from his own (judgment)—
that is, from human sense, not from divine prescript. For, withal, when he has laid down the definitive rule with reference to "the widowed and the unwedded," that they are to "marry if they cannot contain," because "better it is to marry than to burn," he turns around to the other class, and says: "But to the wedded I make official declaration—not indeed I, but the Lord." Thus he shows, by the transfer of his own personality to

the Lord, that what he had said above he had pronounced not in the Lord's person, but in his own: "Better it is to marry than to burn." Now, although that expression pertain to such as *are "apprehended" by the faith* in an unwedded or widowed condition, still, inasmuch as all cling to it with a view to license in the way of marrying, I should wish to give a thorough treatment to the inquiry what kind of good he is pointing out which is "better than" a penalty; which cannot seem good but by comparison with something very bad; so that the reason why "marrying" is good, is that "burning" is worse. "Good" is worthy of the name if it continues to keep that name without comparison, I say not with evil, but even with some second good; so that, even if it *is* compared to some other good, and is by some other cast into the shade, it does nevertheless remain in possession of the name "good." If, however, it is the nature of an *evil* which is the means which compels the predicating "good," it is not so much "good" as a species of inferior evil, which by being obscured by a superior evil is driven to the name of good. Take away, in short, the condition of comparison, so as not to say, "Better it is to marry than to burn;" and I question whether you will have the hardihood to say, "Better it is to marry," not adding what that is which is better. Therefore, what is not *better*, of course is not *good* either; inasmuch as you have taken away and removed the condition of comparison, which, while it makes the thing "better," so compels it to be regarded as "good." "Better it is to marry than to burn" is to be understood in the same way as, "Better it is to lack one eye than two:" if, however, you withdraw from the comparison, it will not be "better" to have one eye, inasmuch as it is not "good" either. Let none therefore catch at a defense (of marriage) from this paragraph, which properly refers to "the unmarried and widows," for whom no (matrimonial) conjunction is yet reckoned: although I hope I have shown that even such must understand the nature of the *permission*.

## Chapter IV. —Further Remarks Upon the Apostle's Language.

However, touching second marriage, we know plainly that the apostle has pronounced: "Thou hast been loosed from a wife; seek not a wife. But if thou shalt marry, thou wilt not sin." Still, as in the former case, he has introduced the order of this discourse too from his personal suggestion, not from a divine precept. But there is a wide difference between a precept of God and a suggestion of man. "Precept of the Lord," says he, "I have not; but I give advice, as having obtained mercy of the Lord to be faithful." In fact, neither in the Gospel nor in Paul's own Epistles will you find a precept of God as the source whence repetition of marriage is permitted. Whence the doctrine that unity (of marriage) must be observed derives confirmation; inasmuch as that which is not found to be *permitted* by the Lord is acknowledged to be *forbidden*. Add (to this consideration) the fact, that even this very introduction of human advice, as if already beginning to reflect upon its own extravagance, immediately restrains and recalls itself, while it subjoins, "However, such shall have pressure of the flesh;" while he says that he "spares them;" while he adds that "the time is wound up," so that "it behooves even such as have wives to act as if they had not;" while he compares the solicitude of the wedded and of the unwedded: for, in teaching, by means of these considerations, the reasons why marrying is not expedient, he dissuades from that to which he had above granted indulgence. And this is the case with regard to first marriage: how much more with regard to second! When, however, he exhorts us to the imitation of his own example, of course, in showing what he *does* wish us to be; that is, continent; he equally declares what he does *not* wish us to be, that is, *in*continent. Thus he, too, while he *wills* one thing, gives no spontaneous or true permission to that which he nills. For had he willed, he would not have *permitted*; nay, rather, he would have *commanded*. "But see again: a woman when her husband is dead, he says, can marry, if she wishes to marry any one, only 'in the Lord.'" Ah! but "happier will she be," he says, "if she shall remain permanently as she is, according to my opinion. I think, moreover, I too have the Spirit of God." We see two advices: that whereby, above, he grants the indulgence of marrying; and that whereby, just afterwards, he teaches continence with regard to marrying. "To which, then," you say, "shall we assent?" Look at them carefully, and choose. In granting indulgence, he alleges the advice of a prudent *man*; in enjoining continence, he affirms the advice of the Holy Spirit. Follow the admonition which has divinity for its patron. It is true that believers likewise "have the Spirit of God;" but not all believers are apostles. When then, he who had called himself a "believer," added thereafter that he "had the Spirit of God," which no one would doubt even in the case of an (ordinary) believer; his reason for saying so was, that he might reassert for himself apostolic dignity. For apostles have the Holy Spirit properly, who have Him fully, in the operations of prophecy, and the efficacy of (healing) virtues, and the evidences of tongues; not partially, as all others have. Thus he attached the Holy Spirit's authority to that form (of advice) to which he willed us rather to attend; and forthwith it became not an *advice* of the Holy Spirit, but, in consideration of His majesty, a *precept*.

Chapter V.—Unity of Marriage Taught by Its First Institution, and by the Apostle's Application of that Primal Type to Christ and the Church.

For the laying down of the law of once marrying, the very origin of the human race is our authority; witnessing as it emphatically does what God constituted in the beginning for a type to be examined with care by posterity. For when He had molded man, and had foreseen that a peer was necessary for him, He borrowed from his ribs one, and fashioned for him one woman; whereas, of course, neither the Artificer nor the material would have been insufficient (for the creation of more). There were more ribs in Adam, and hands that knew no weariness in God; but not more wives in the eye of God. And accordingly the man of God, Adam, and the woman of God, Eve, discharging mutually (the duties of) one marriage, sanctioned for mankind a type by (the considerations of) the authoritative precedent of their origin and the primal will of God. Finally, "there shall be," said He, "two in one flesh," not three nor four. On any other hypothesis, there would no longer be "one flesh," nor "two (joined) into one flesh." These will be so, if the conjunction and the growing together in unity take place *once for all*. If, however, (it take place) a second time, or oftener, immediately (the flesh) ceases to be "one," and there will not be "two (joined) into one flesh," but plainly one rib (divided) into more. But when the apostle interprets, "The two shall be (joined) into one flesh" of the Church and Christ, according to the spiritual nuptials of the Church and Christ (for Christ is one, and one is His Church), we are bound to recognize a duplication and additional enforcement for *us* of the law of unity of marriage, not only in accordance with the foundation of our race, but in accordance with the sacrament of Christ. From one marriage do we derive our origin in each case; carnally in Adam, spiritually in Christ. The two births combine in laying down one prescriptive rule of monogamy. In regard of each of the two, is he degenerate who transgresses the limit of monogamy. Plurality of marriage began with an accursed man. Lamech was the first who, by marrying himself to two women, caused *three* to be (joined) "into one flesh."

Chapter VI. —The Objection from the Polygamy of the Patriarchs Answered.

"But withal the blessed patriarchs," you say, "made mingled alliances not only with more wives (than one), but with concubines likewise." Shall that, then, make it lawful for us also to marry without limit? I grant that it will, if there still remain types—sacraments of something future—for your nuptials to figure; or if even now there is room for that command, "Grow and multiply;" that is, if no other command has yet supervened: "The time is already wound up; it remains that both they who have wives act as if they had not:" for, of course, by enjoining continence, and restraining concubitance, the seminary of our race, (this latter command) has abolished that "Grow and multiply." As I think, moreover, each pronouncement and arrangement is (the act) of one and the same God; who did then indeed, in the beginning, send forth a sowing of the race by an indulgent laxity granted to the reins of connubial alliances, until the world should be replenished, until the material of the new discipline should attain to forwardness: now, however, at the extreme boundaries of the times, has checked (the command) which He had sent out, and recalled the indulgence which He had granted; not without a reasonable ground for the extension (of that indulgence) in the beginning, and the limitation of it in the end. Laxity is always allowed to the beginning (of things). The reason why anyone plants a wood and lets it grow, is that at his own time he may cut it. The wood was the old order, which is being pruned down by the new Gospel, in which withal "the axe has been laid at the roots." So, too, "Eye for eye, and tooth for tooth," has now grown old, ever since "Let none render evil for evil" grew young. I think, moreover, that even with a view to *human* institutions and decrees, things later prevail over things primitive.

Chapter VII. —Even the Old Discipline Was Not Without Precedents to Enforce Monogamy. But in This as in Other Respects, the New Has Brought in a Higher Perfection.

Why, moreover, should we not rather recognize, from among (the store of) primitive precedents, those which communicate with the later (order of things) in respect of discipline, and transmit to novelty the typical form of antiquity? For look, in the old law I find the pruning-knife applied to the license of repeated marriage. There is a caution in Leviticus: "My priests shall not pluralize marriages." I may affirm even that that is plural which is not once for all. That which is not unity is number. In short, after unity begins number. Unity, moreover, is everything which is once for all. But for Christ was reserved, as in all other points so in this also, the "fulfilling of the law." Thence, therefore, among *us* the prescript is more fully and more carefully laid down, that they who are chosen into the sacerdotal order must be men of one marriage; which rule is so rigidly observed, that I remember some removed from their office for digamy. But you will say, "Then all others may (marry more than once), whom he excepts." Vain shall we be if we think that what is not

lawful for priests is lawful for laics. Are not even we laics priests? It is written: "A kingdom also, and priests to His God and Father, hath He made us." It is the authority of the Church, and the honor which has acquired sanctity through the joint session of the Order, which has established the difference between the Order and the laity. Accordingly, where there is no joint session of the ecclesiastical Order, you offer, and baptize, and are priest, alone for yourself. But where three are, a church is, albeit they be laics. For each individual lives by his own faith, nor is there exception of persons with God; since it is not hearers of the law who are justified by the Lord, but doers, according to what the apostle withal says. Therefore, if you have the *right* of a priest in your own person, in cases of

necessity, it behooves you to have likewise the *discipline* of a priest whenever it may be necessary to have the right of a priest. If you are a digamist, do you baptize? If you are a digamist, do you offer? How much more capital (a crime) is it for a digamist laic to act as a priest, when the priest himself, if he turns digamist, is deprived of the power of acting the priest! "But to necessity," you say, "indulgence is granted." No necessity is excusable which is avoidable. In a word, shun to be found guilty of digamy, and you do not expose yourself to the necessity of administering what a digamist may not lawfully administer. God wills us all to be so conditioned, as to be ready at all times and places to undertake (the duties of) His sacraments. There is "one God, one faith," one discipline too. So truly is this the case, that unless the laics as well observe the rules which are to guide the choice of presbyters, how will there be presbyters at all, who are chosen to that office from among the laics? Hence we are bound to contend that the command to abstain from second marriage relates *first* to the laic; so long as no other can be a presbyter than a laic, provided he have been *once for all* a husband.

## Chapter VIII. —If It Be Granted that Second Marriage is Lawful, Yet All Things Lawful Are Not Expedient.

Let it now be granted that repetition of marriage is lawful, if everything which is lawful is good. The same apostle exclaims: "All things are lawful, but all are not profitable." Pray, can what is "not profitable" be called good? If even things which do not make for salvation are "lawful," it follows that even things which are not good are "lawful." But what will it be your duty rather to choose; that which is good because it is "lawful," or that which is so because it is "profitable?" A wide difference I take to exist between "license" and salvation. Concerning the "good" it is not said "it is lawful;" inasmuch as "good" does not expect to be permitted, but to be assumed. But that is "permitted" about which a doubt exists whether it be "good;" which may likewise *not* be permitted, if it have not some first (extrinsic) cause of its being:—inasmuch as it is *on account of the danger of incontinence* that second marriage, (for instance), is permitted:—because, unless the "license" of some not (absolutely) good thing were subject (so our choice), there were no means of proving who rendered a willing obedience to the Divine will, and who to his own power; which of us follows presentiality, and which embraces the opportunity of license. "Licence," for the most part, is a trial of discipline; since it is through trial that discipline is proved, and through "license" that trial operates. Thus it comes to pass that "all things are lawful, but not all are expedient," so long as (it remains true that) whoever has a "permission" granted is (thereby) tried, and is (consequently) judged during the process of trial in (the case of the particular) "permission." Apostles, withal, had a "license" to marry, and lead wives about (with them). They had a "license," too, to "live by the Gospel." But he who, when occasion required, "did not use this right," provokes us to imitate his own example; teaching us that our probation consists in that wherein "license" has laid the groundwork for the experimental proof of abstinence.

Chapter IX. —Second Marriage a Species of Adultery, Marriage Itself Impugned, as Akin to Adultery.

If we look deeply into his meanings, and interpret them, second marriage will have to be termed no other than a species of fornication. For, since he says that married persons make this their solicitude, "how to please one another" (not, of course, *morally*, for a good solicitude he would not impugn); and (since), he wishes them to be understood to be solicitous about dress, and ornament, and every kind of personal attraction, with a view to increasing their power of allurement; (since), moreover, to please by personal beauty and dress is the genius of carnal concupiscence, which again is the cause of fornication: pray, does second marriage seem to you to border upon fornication, since in it are detected those ingredients which are appropriate to fornication? The Lord Himself said, "Whoever has seen a woman with a view to concupiscence has already violated her in his heart." But has he who has seen her with a view to marriage done so less or more? What if he has even married her? —which he would not do had he not desired her with a view to marriage, and seen her with a view to concupiscence; unless it is possible for a wife to be married whom you have not seen or desired. I grant it makes a wide difference whether a married man or an unmarried desire another woman. Every woman, (however), even to an unmarried man, is "another," so long as she belongs to someone else; nor yet is the mean through which she becomes a married woman any other than that through which withal (she becomes) an adulteress. It is laws which seem to make the difference between marriage and fornication; through diversity of illicitness, not through the nature of the thing itself. Besides, what is the thing which takes place in all men and women to produce marriage and fornication? Commixture of the flesh, of course; the concupiscence whereof the Lord put on the same footing with fornication. "Then," says (someone), "are you by this time destroying first—that is, single—marriage too?" And (if so) not without reason; inasmuch as it, too, consists of that which is the essence of fornication. Accordingly, the best thing for a man is not to touch a woman; and accordingly the virgin's is the principal sanctity, because it is free from affinity with fornication. And since these considerations may be advanced, even in the case of first and single marriage, to forward the cause of continence, how much more will they afford a prejudgment for refusing second marriage? Be thankful if God has once for all granted you indulgence to marry. Thankful, moreover, you will be if you know not that He has granted you that indulgence a second time. But you abuse indulgence if you avail yourself of it without moderation. Moderation is understood (to be derived) from *modus*, a limit. It does not suffice you to have fallen back, by marrying, from that highest grade of immaculate virginity; but you roll yourself down into yet a third, and into a fourth,

and perhaps into more, after you have failed to be continent in the second stage; inasmuch as he who has treated about contracting second marriages has not willed to prohibit even more. Marry we, therefore, daily. And marrying, let us be overtaken by the last day, like Sodom and Gomorrah; that day when the "woe" pronounced over "such as are with child
and giving suck" shall be fulfilled, that is, over the married and the incontinent: for from marriage result wombs, and breasts, and infants. And when an end of marrying? I believe after the end of living!

Chapter X.—Application of the Subject. Advantages of Widowhood.

Renounce we things carnal, that we may at length bear fruits spiritual. Seize the opportunity—albeit not earnestly desired, yet favorable—of not having any one to whom to pay a debt, and by whom to be (yourself) repaid! You have ceased to be a debtor. Happy man! You have released your debtor; sustain the loss. What if you come to feel that what we have called a loss is a gain? For continence will be a mean whereby you will traffic in a mighty substance of sanctity; by parsimony of the flesh you will gain the Spirit. For let us ponder over our conscience itself, (to see) how different a man feels himself when he chances to be deprived of his wife. He savors spiritually. If he is making prayer to the Lord, he is near heaven. If he is bending over the Scriptures, he is "wholly in them." If he is singing a psalm, he satisfies himself. If he is adjuring a demon, he is confident in himself. Accordingly,
the apostle added (the recommendation of) a temporary abstinence for the sake of adding an efficacy to prayers, that we might know that what is profitable "for a time" should be always practiced by us, that it may be always profitable. Daily, every moment, prayer is necessary to men; of course continence (is so) too, since prayer is necessary. Prayer proceeds from conscience. If the conscience blush, prayer blushes. It is the spirit which conducts prayer to God. If the

spirit be self-accused of a blushing conscience, how will it have the hardihood to conduct prayer to the altar; seeing that, if prayer blush, the holy minister (of prayer) itself is suffused too? For there is a prophetic utterance of the Old Testament: "Holy shall ye be, because God is holy;" and again: "With the holy thou shalt be sanctified; and with the innocent man thou shalt be innocent; and with the elect, elect." For it is our duty so to walk in the Lord's discipline as is "worthy," not according to the filthy concupiscences of the flesh. For so, too, does the apostle say, that "to savor according to the flesh is death, but to savor according to the spirit is life eternal in Jesus Christ our Lord." Again, through the holy prophetess Prisca the Gospel is thus preached: that "the holy minister knows how to minister sanctity." "For purity," says she, "is harmonious, and they see visions; and, turning their face downward, they even hear manifest voices, as salutary as they are withal secret." If this dulling (of the spiritual faculties), even when the carnal nature is allowed room for exercise in first marriage, averts the Holy Spirit; how much more when it is brought into play in second marriage!

## Chapter XI. —The More the Wives, the Greater the Distraction of the Spirit.

For (in that case) the shame is double; inasmuch as, in second marriage, two wives beset the same husband—one in spirit, one in flesh. For the first wife you cannot hate, for whom you retain an even more religious affection, as being already received into the Lord's presence; for whose spirit you make request; for whom you render annual oblations. Will you stand, then, before the Lord with as many wives as you commemorate in prayer; and will you offer for two; and will you commend those two (to God) by the ministry of a priest ordained (to his sacred office) on the score of monogamy, or else consecrated (thereto) on the score even of virginity, surrounded by widows married but to one husband? And will your sacrifice ascend with unabashed front, and—among all the other (graces) of a good mind—will you request for yourself and for your wife chastity?

Chapter XII. —Excuses Commonly Urged in Defense of Second Marriage. Their Futility, especially in the Case of Christians, Pointed Out.

I am aware of the excuses by which we color our insatiable carnal appetite. Our pretexts are: the necessities of props to lean on; a house to be managed; a family to be governed; chests and keys to be guarded; the wool-spinning to be dispensed; food to be attended to; cares to be generally lessened. Of course the houses of none but married men
fare well! The families of celibates, the estates of eunuchs, the fortunes of military men, or of such as travel without wives, have gone to rack and ruin! For are not we, too, soldiers?
Soldiers, indeed, subject to all the stricter discipline, that we are subject to so great a General? Are not we, too, travelers in this world? Why moreover, Christian, are you so conditioned, that you cannot (so travel) without a wife? "In my present (widowed) state, too, a consort in domestic works is necessary." (Then) take some spiritual wife. Take to
yourself from among the widows one fair in faith, dowered with poverty, sealed with age. You will (thus) make a good marriage. A plurality of *such* wives is pleasing to God. "But Christians concern themselves about posterity"—to whom there is no to-morrow! Shall the servant of God yearn after heirs, who has disinherited himself from the world? And is
it to be a reason for a man to repeat marriage, if from his first (marriage) he have no children? And shall he thus have, as the first benefit (resulting therefrom), this, that he should desire longer life, when the apostle himself is in haste to be "with the Lord?" Assuredly, most free will he be from encumbrance in persecutions, most constant in martyrdoms, most prompt in distributions of his goods, most temperate in acquisitions;

lastly, undistracted by cares will he die, when he has left children behind him—perhaps to perform the last rites over his grave! Is it then, perchance, in forecast for the commonwealth that such (marriages) are contracted? for fear the States fail, if no rising generations be trained up? for fear the rights of law, for fear the branches of commerce, sink quite into decay? for fear the temples be quite forsaken? for fear there be none to raise the acclaim, "The lion for the Christians?"—for these are the acclaims which they desire to hear who go in quest of offspring! Let the well-known burdensomeness of children—especially in *our* case—suffice to counsel widowhood: (children) whom men are compelled by laws to undertake (the charge of); because no wise man would ever willingly have desired sons! What, then, will you do if you succeed in filling your new wife with your own conscientious scruples? Are you to dissolve the conception by aid of drugs? I think to *us* it is no more lawful to hurt (a child) in process of birth, than one (already) born. But perhaps at that time of your wife's pregnancy you will have the hardihood to beg from God a remedy for so grave a solicitate, which, when it lay in your own power, you refused? Some (naturally) barren woman, I suppose, or (some woman) of an age already feeling the chill of years, will be the object of your forecasting search. A course prudent enough, and, above all, worthy of a believer! For there is no woman whom we have believed to have borne (a child) when barren or old, when God so willed! which he is all the more likely to do if any one, by the presumption of this foresight of his own, provoke emulation on the part of God. In fine, we know a case among our brethren, in which one of them took a barren woman in second marriage for his daughter's sake, and became as well for the second time a father as for the second time a husband.

Chapter XIII. —Examples from Among the Heathen, as Well as from the Church, to Enforce the Foregoing Exhortation.

To this my exhortation, best beloved brother, there are added even heathenish examples; which have often been set by ourselves as well (as by others) in evidence, when anything good and pleasing to God is, even among "strangers," recognized and honored with a testimony. In short, monogamy among the heathen is so held in highest honor, that even virgins, when legitimately marrying, have a woman never married but once appointed them as brides woman; and if *you say that* "this is for the sake of the omen," of course it is for the sake of a *good* omen; again, that in some solemnities and official functions, single-husband hood takes the precedence: at all events, the wife of a Flamen must be but once married, which is the law of the Flamen (himself) too. For the fact that the chief pontiff himself must not iterate marriage is, of course, a glory to monogamy. When, however, Satan affects God's sacraments, it is a challenge to us; nay, rather, a cause for blushing, if we are slow to exhibit to God a continence which some render to the devil, by perpetuity sometimes of virginity, sometimes of widowhood. We have heard of Vesta's virgins, and Juno's at the town of Achaia, and Apollo's among the Delphians, and Minerva's and Diana's in some places. We have heard, too, of continent *men*, and (among others) the priests of the famous Egyptian bull: women, moreover, (dedicated) to the African Ceres, in whose honor they even spontaneously abdicate matrimony, and so live to old age, shunning thenceforward all contact with males, even so much as the kisses of their sons. The devil, forsooth, has discovered, after voluptuousness, even a chastity which shall work perdition; that the guilt may be all the deeper of the Christian who refuses the chastity which helps to salvation! A testimony to us shall be, too, some of heathendom's women, who have won renown for their obstinate persistence in single-husband

hood: some Dido, (for instance), who, refugee as she was on alien soil, when she ought rather to have desired, without any external solicitation, marriage with a king, did yet, for fear of experiencing a second union, prefer, contrariwise,
to "burn" rather than to "marry;" or the famous Lucretia, who, albeit it was but once, by force, and against her will, that she had suffered a strange man, washed her stained flesh in her own blood, lest she should live, when no longer single-husbanded in her own esteem! A little more care will furnish you with more examples from our own (sisters); and *those*
indeed, superior to the others, inasmuch as it is a greater thing to live in chastity than to die for it. Easier it is to lay down your life because you have lost a blessing, than to keep by living
that for which you would rather die outright. How many men, therefore, and how many women, in Ecclesiastical Orders, owe their position to continence, who have preferred to be wedded to God; who have restored the honor of their flesh, and who have already dedicated themselves as sons of that (future) age, by slaying in themselves the concupiscence of lust, and that whole (propensity) which could not be admitted within Paradise! Whence it is presumable that such as shall wish to be received within Paradise, ought at last to begin to cease from that thing from which Paradise is intact.

## Elucidation.

(Albeit they be laics, p. 54.)

In the tract on *Baptism* Tertullian uses language implying that three persons compose a Church. But here we find it much more strongly pronounced,—*Ubi tres, Ecclesia est, licet Laici.* The question of lay-baptism we may leave till we come to Cyprian, only noting here, that, while Cyprian abjures his "master" on this point, his adversary, the Bishop of Rome, adopts Tertullian's principle in so far. But, in view of

Matt. xix. 20, surely we may all allow that three are a *quorum* when so "gathered together in Christ's name," albeit not for all purposes. Three women may claim the Savior's promise when lawfully met together for social devotions, nor can it be denied that they have a share in the priesthood of the "peculiar people." So, too, even of three pious children. But it does not follow that they are a church *for all purposes*, —preaching, celebrating sacraments, ordaining, and the like. The late Dean Stanley was fond of this passage of Tertullian, but obviously it might be abused to encourage a state of things which all orderly and organized systems of religion must necessarily discard. On p. 58 there is a reference, apparently, to *deaconesses* as "women in Ecclesiastical Orders."

www.ingramcontent.com/pod-product-compliance
Lightning Source LLC
Chambersburg PA
CBHW052046070526
44584CB00018B/2634